*Commissioned for and premiered at the Memorial Concert
honoring the renowned concert artist, Tom Hazleton*

From Earth to Glory

CAROLYN HAMLIN
(ASCAP)

Sw. Viola 8', Gedeckt 8', Principal 4', Piccolo 2', Mix. IV
Gt.   Diapason 8', Octave 4', Spitzflote 4', Sw. to Gt. 8'
Ch. Gedeckt 8', Principal 4', Koppelflute 4'
Ped. Bourdon 16', Violone 16', Octave 8', Choral Bass 4',
     Bassoon 16', Gt. to Ped. 8', Sw. to Ped. 8'

With grandeur ♩ = 98

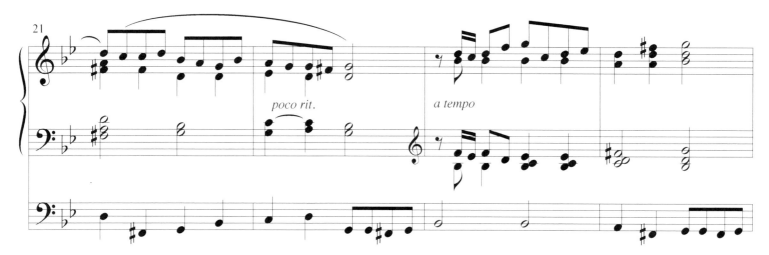

Trio Reg. I
Sw. Viola 8', Viola Celeste 8', Flute Celeste II 8', Vox Humana 8', Trem.
Gt.   Gamba 8', Trem., Sw. to Gt. 16', 8', 4', Ch. to Gt. 8'
Ch. Erzahler 16', 8', Erzahler Celeste 8', Trem.
Ped. Bourdon 32', 16', Violone 16', Sw. to Ped. 8', Ch. to Ped. 8'

With much expression ♩ = 94

Trio Reg. II
Sw. Viola 8', Bourdon 8', Principal 4', Mix. IV
Gt.   Diapason 8', Harmonic Flute 8', Octave 4', Fifteenth 2', Mix. IV, Sw. to Gt. 8', Ch. to Gt. 8'
Ch. Gedeckt 8', Principal 4', Octave 2', Quintflute 1⅓', Sw. to Ch. 8'
Ped. Bourdon 16', Violone 16', Waldhorn 16', Gt. to Ped. 8', Sw. to Ped. 8'

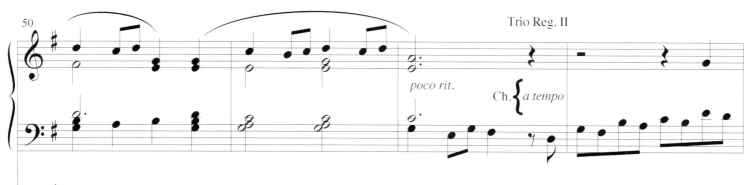

Opening Registration

Unhurried

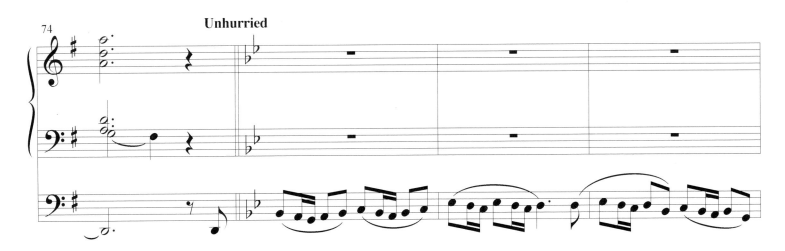

To opening registration add:

Sw. Bassoon 16', Trumpet 8', Clarion 4'
Gt. Scharf III
Ch. Zimbell III
Ped. Diapason 16', Bombarde 16', Trompette 8'

With grandeur ♩ = 98

poco rit.

a tempo

poco rit.

a tempo

Full Organ with Reeds

play flourish as quickly as possible